I like Ice Cream!

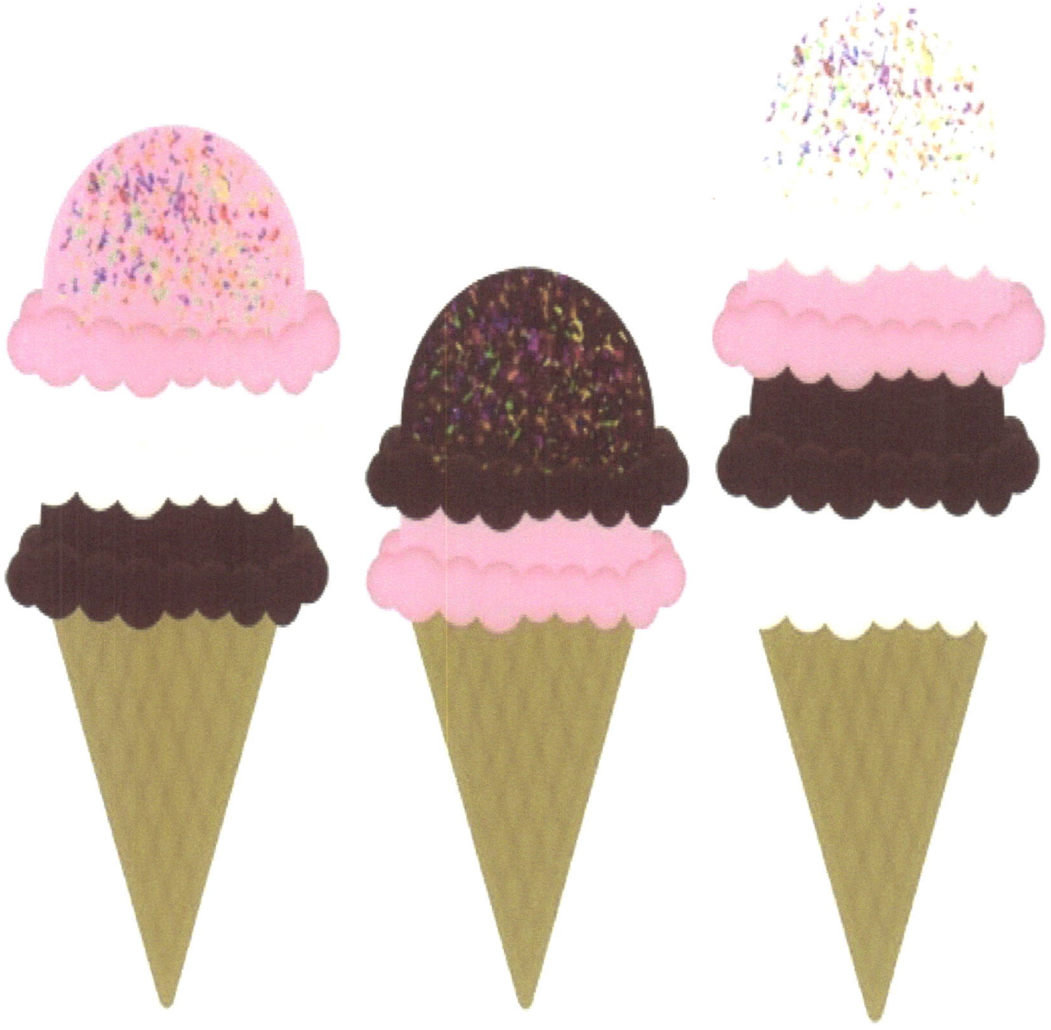

Written By: Melissa L. Bryant

I dedicate this book to my children, nieces, nephews, god-children and to all the children around the world. I pray you all enjoy this book of ice cream. I love ice cream! What about you? Ice Cream is good when you're sick. Thanks for all the love and support. God bless and the best is yet to come.

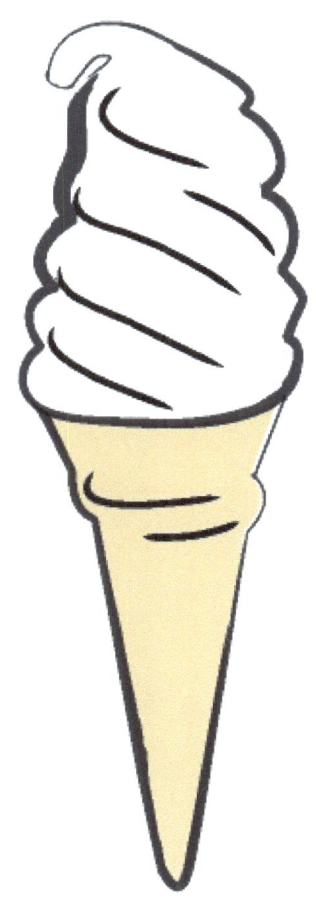

I love Vanilla Ice Cream. What about you?

I like Strawberry Ice cream. What about you?

I love Chocolate Ice Cream. What about you?

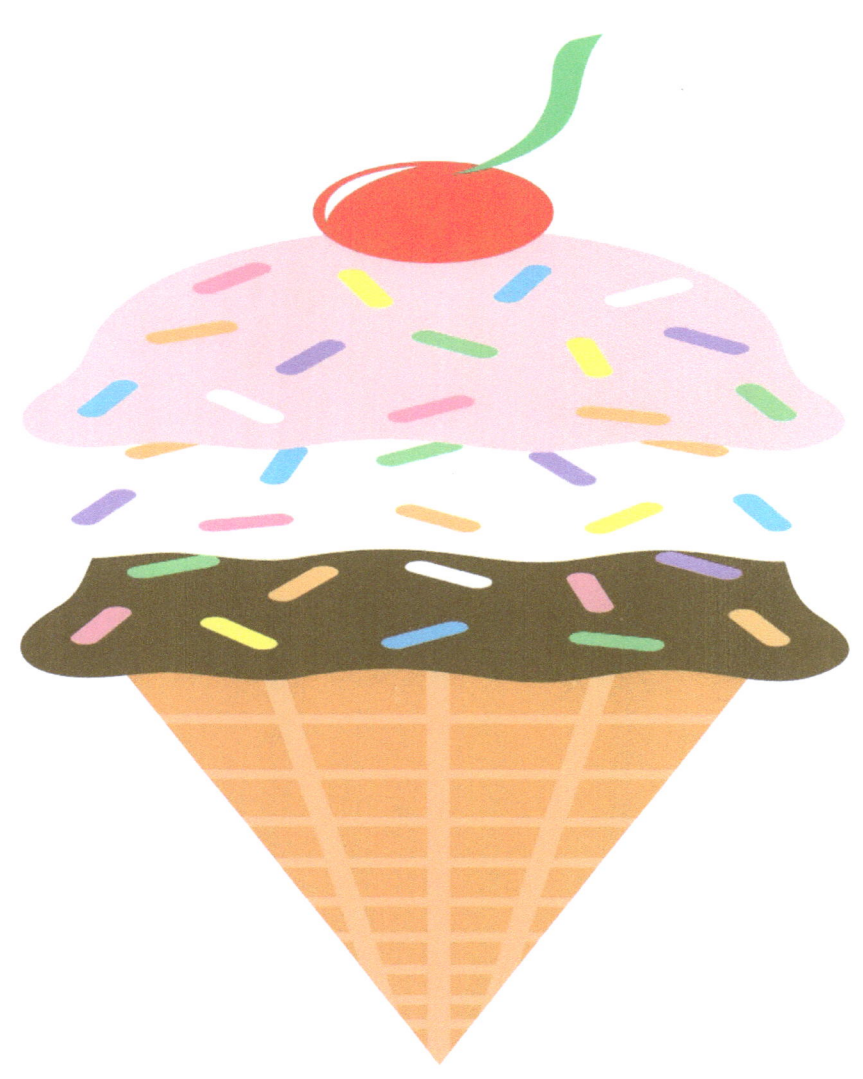

I like Chocolate, Vanilla and Strawberry with sprinkles and a cherry on top. What about you?

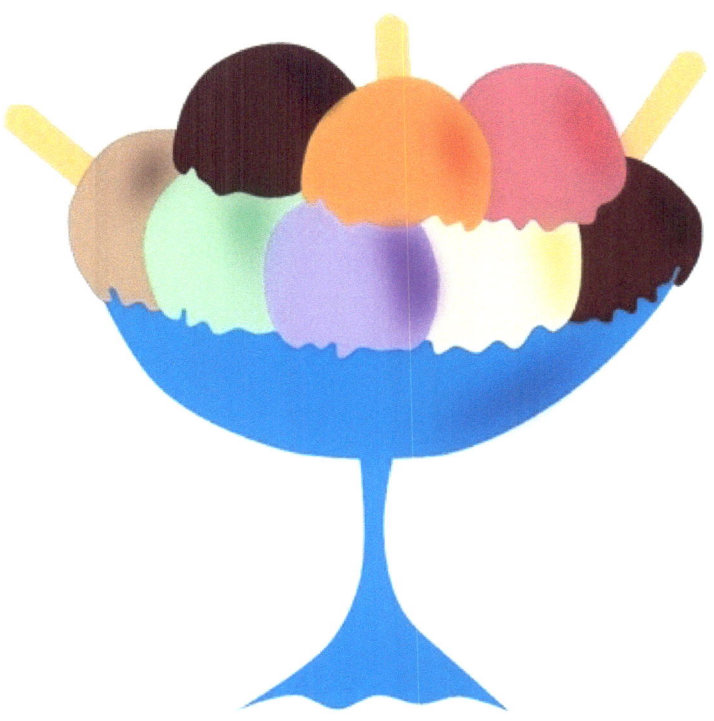

I like different ice cream favors. What about you?

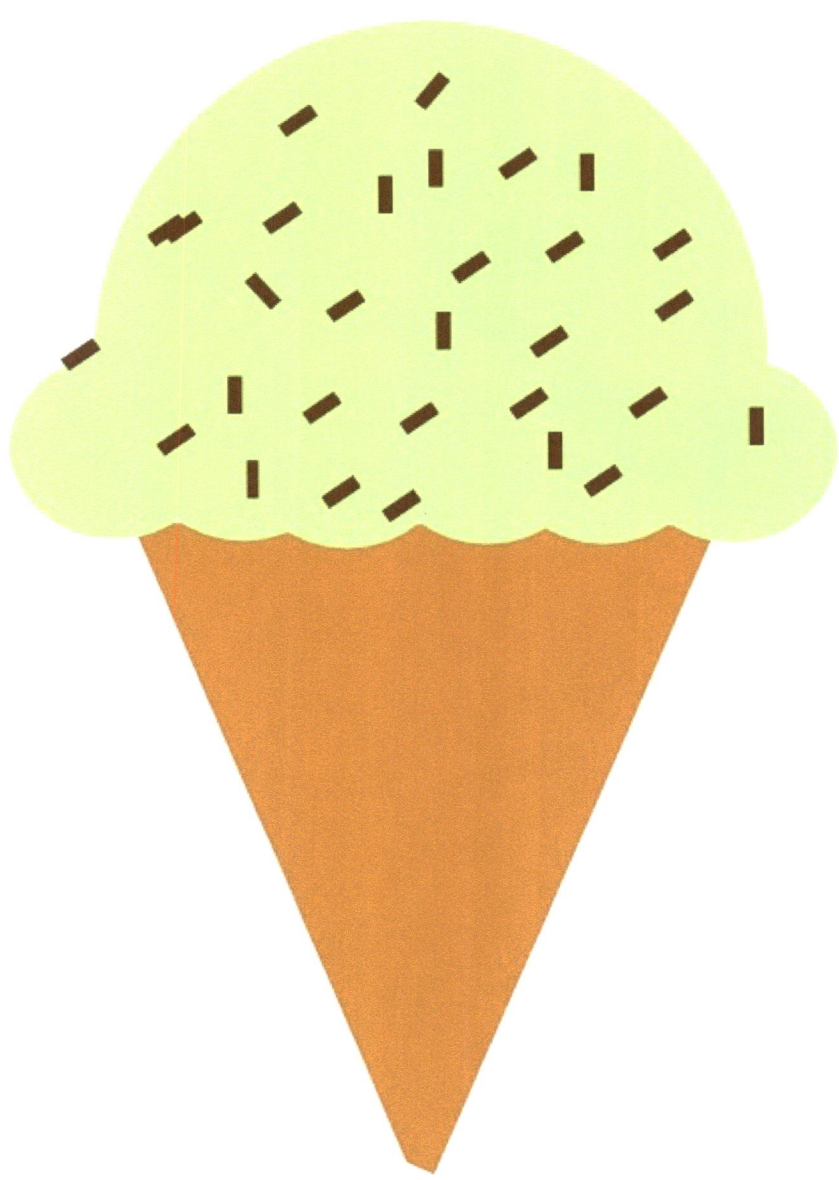

I like Green Ice Cream with sprinkles on it. What about you?

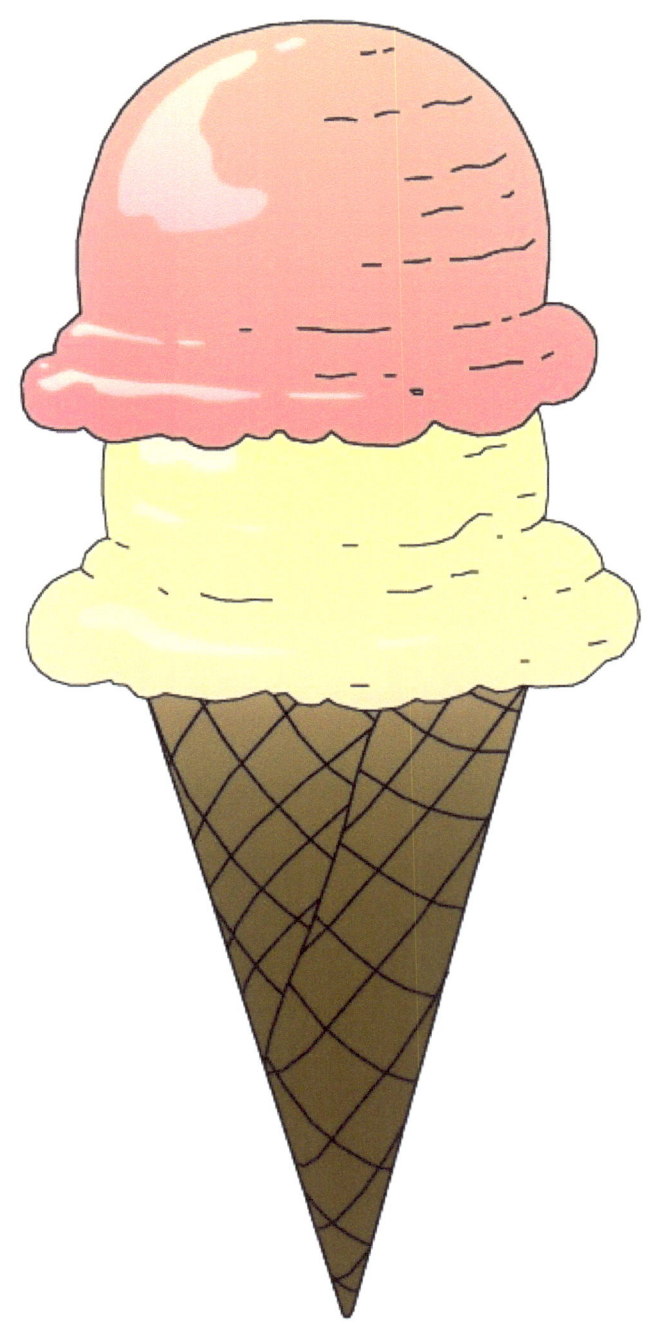

I like two scoop ice cream cones. What about you?

I like Vanilla and Strawberry Ice Cream. What about you?

I like Ice Cream with sprinkles and a cherry on the top. What about you?

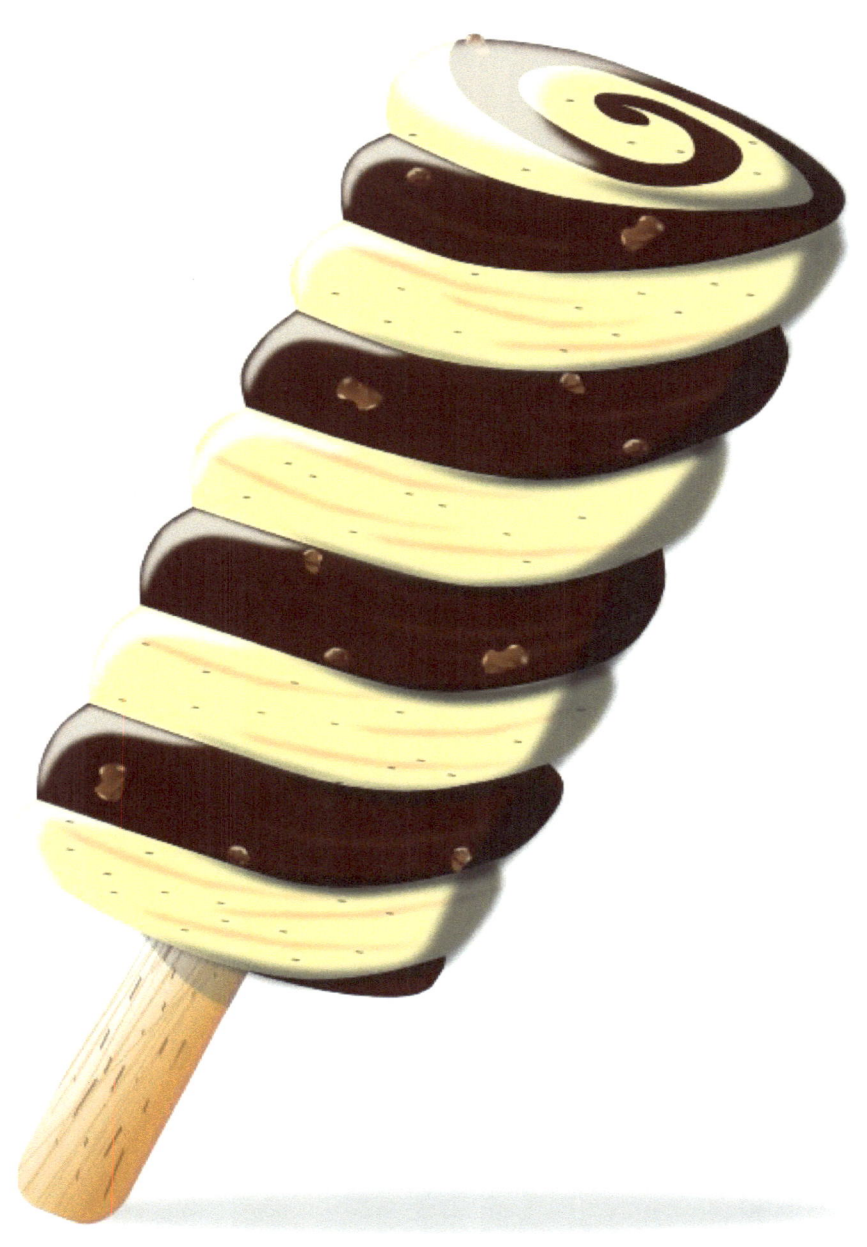

I like Twisted Ice Cream. What about you?

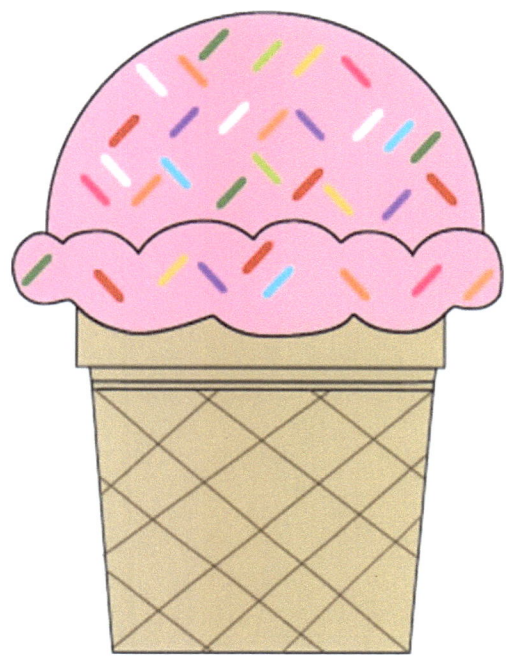

I like Strawberry with sprinkles. What about you?

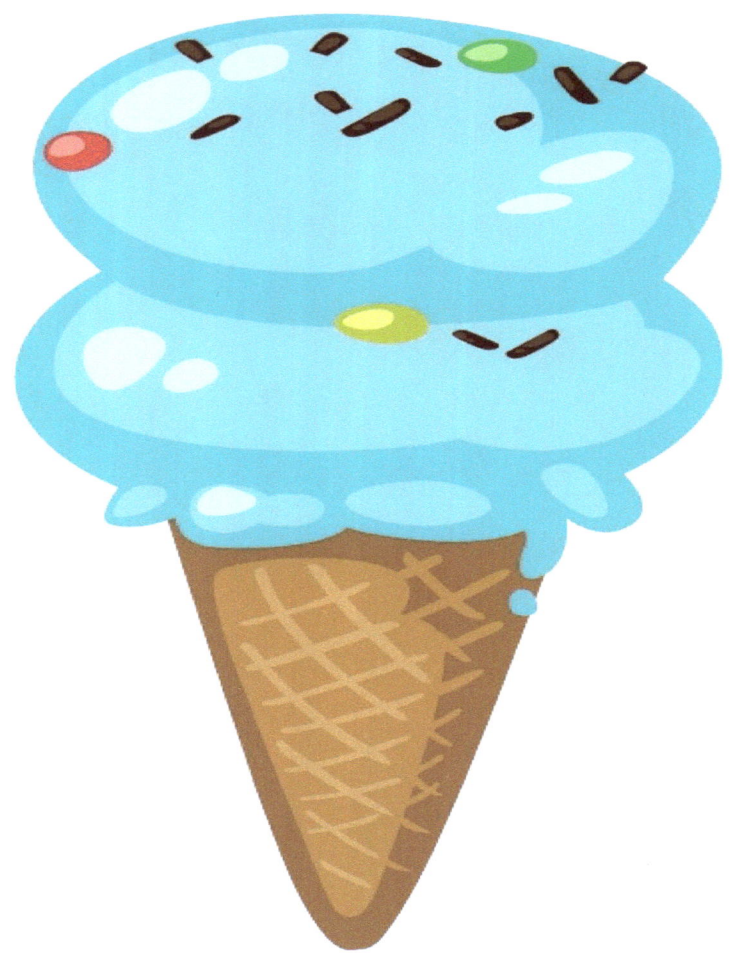

I love Bubblegum Ice Cream. What about you?

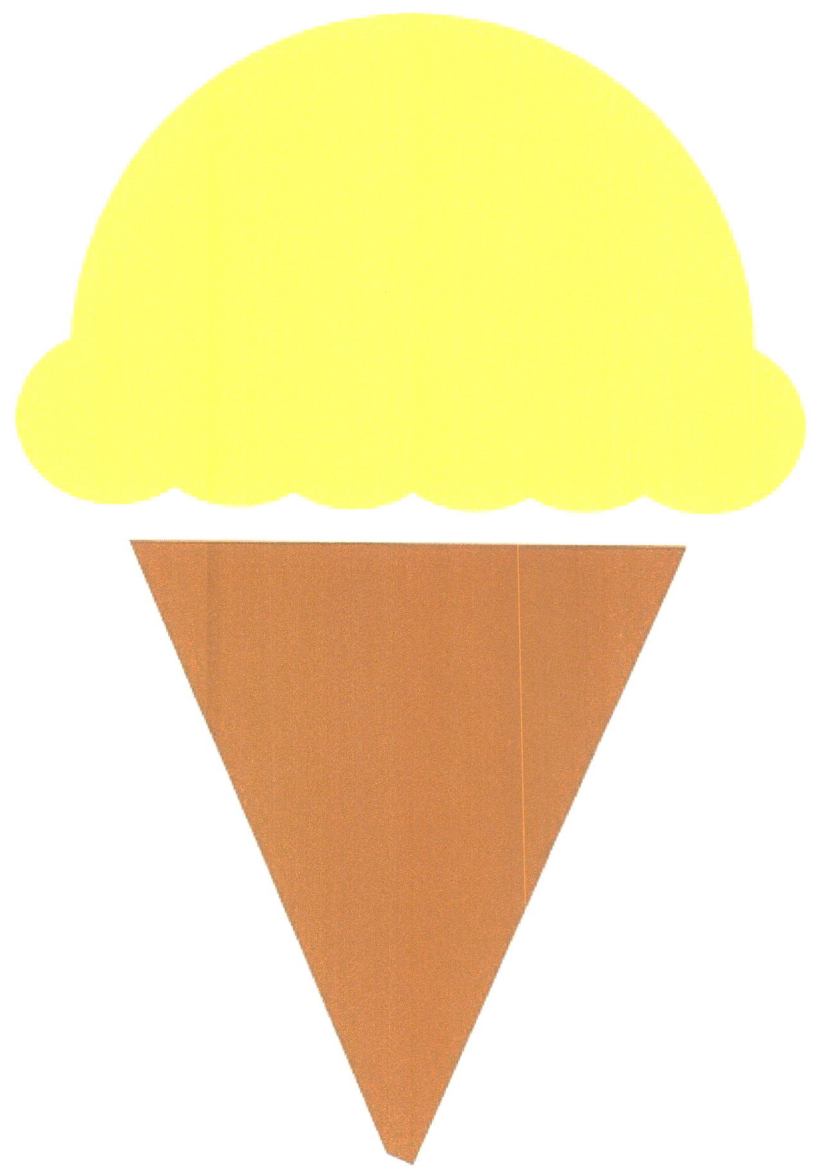

I like Yellow Ice Cream. What about you?

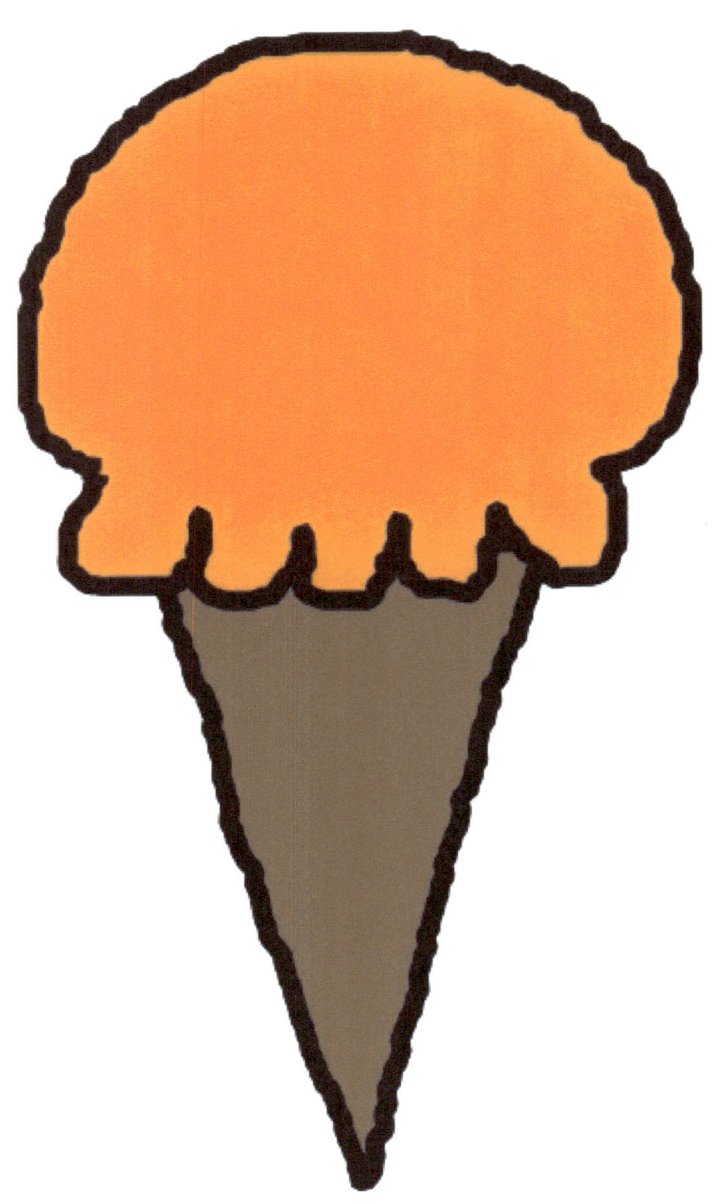

I like Mango Ice Cream. What about you?

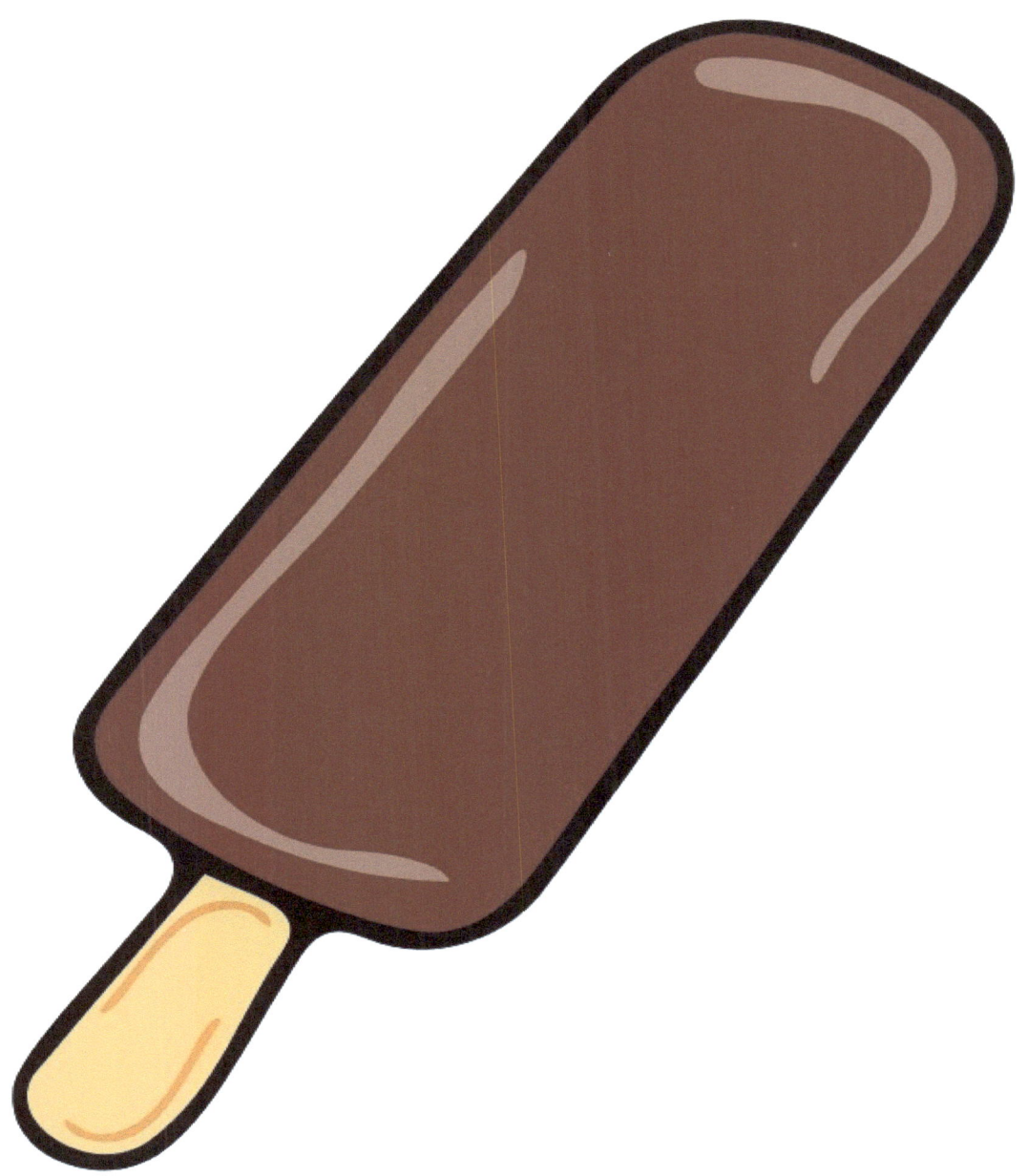

I love Chocolate Popsicle Ice Cream. What about you?

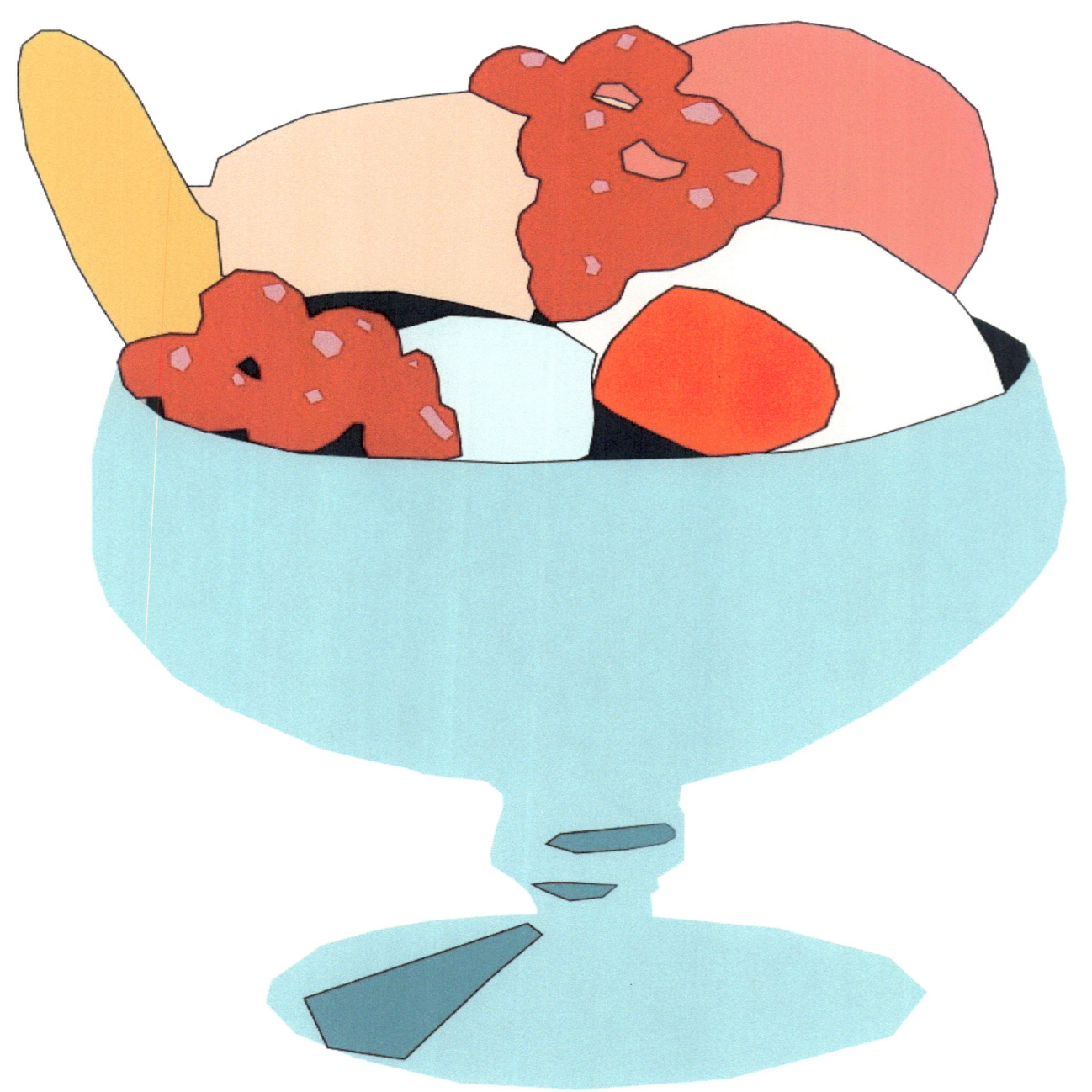

I like Ice Cream cup. What about you?

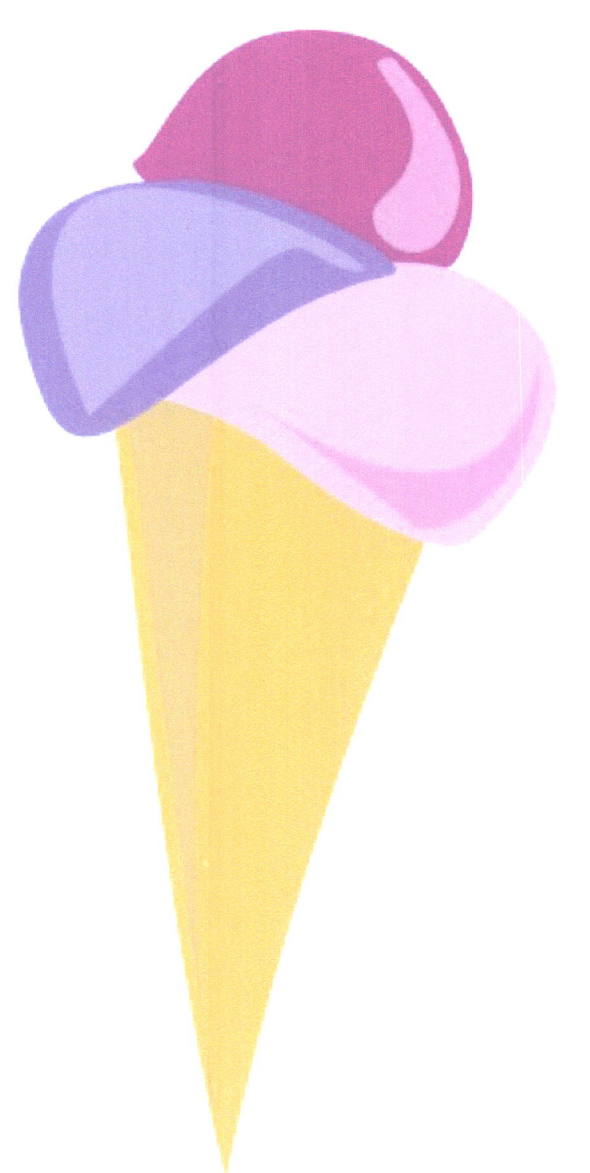

I love different favors of Ice Cream. What about you?

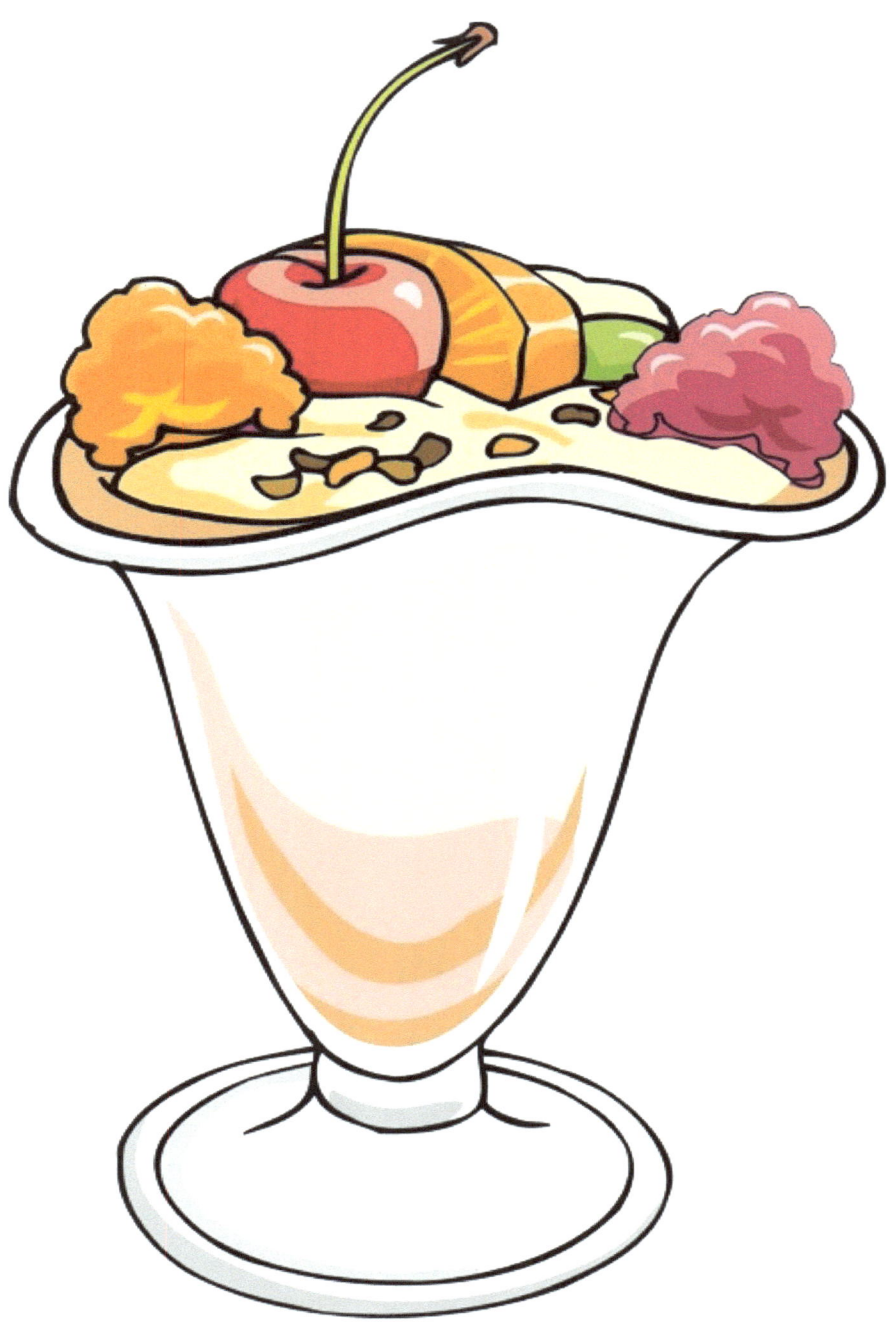

I love Ice Cream Sundae. What about you?

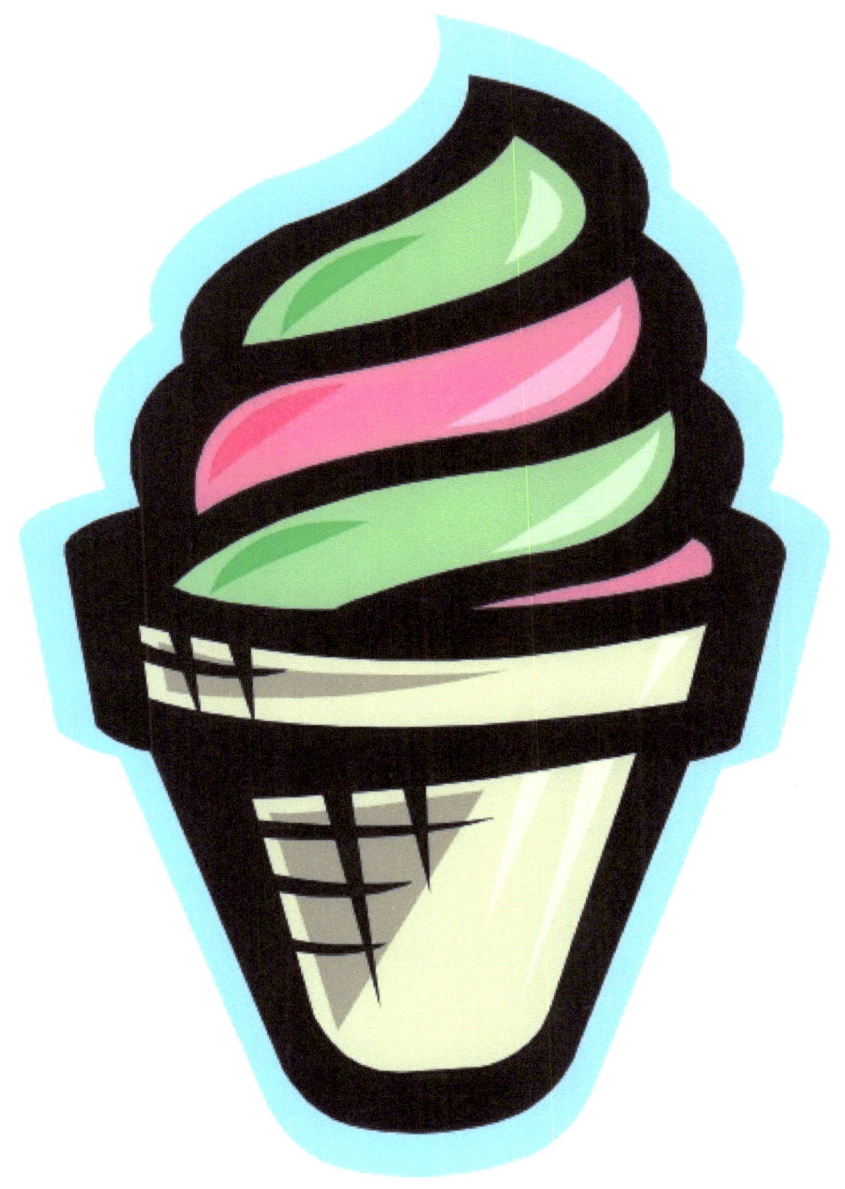

I love Green and Pink Ice Cream. What about you?

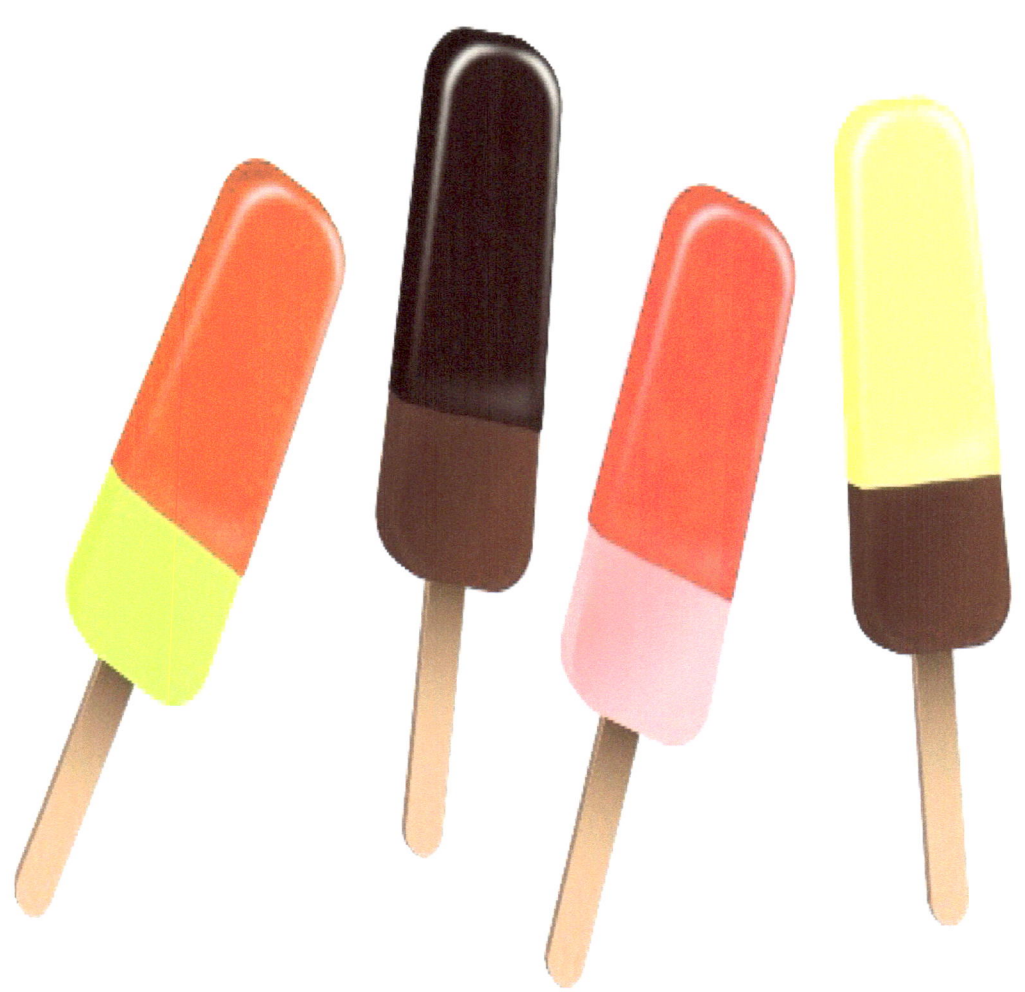

I love colorful Popsicle Ice Cream. What about you?

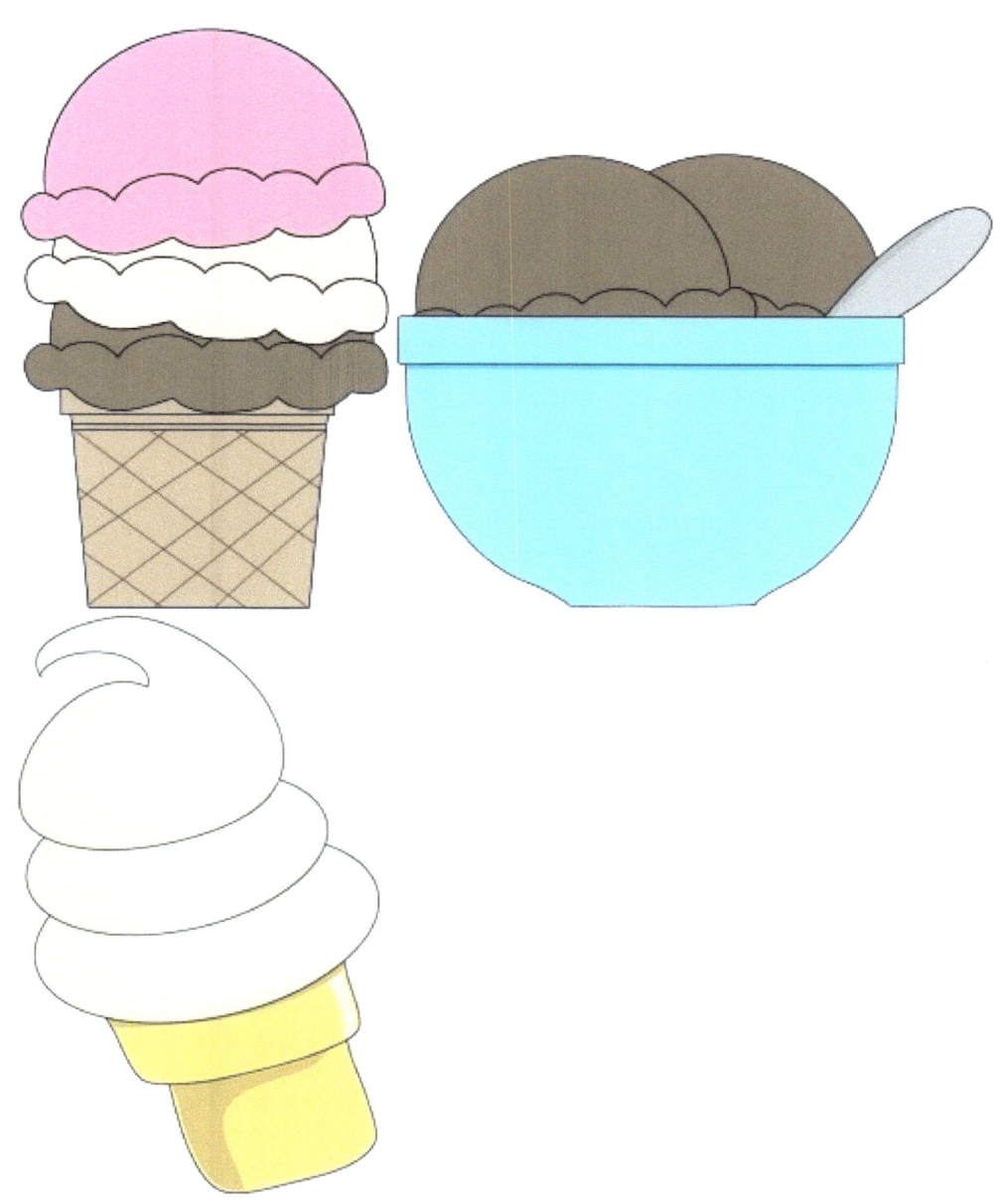

I love different type of Ice Creams. What about you?